SEPTEMBER
PATTERNS, PROJECTS & PLANS

by
Imogene Forte

Incentive Publications, Inc.
Nashville, Tennessee

Illustrated by Gayle Seaberg Harvey
Cover by Susan Eaddy
Edited by Sally Sharpe

ISBN 0-86530-125-5

Table of Contents

PREFACE

September — a month of new beginnings

SEPTEMBER...

...A TIME of seasonal change — leaves turn brilliant colors and fall from trees, summer flowers fade and autumn flowers blossom, hot weather gives way to cool breezes, puffy white clouds dot brilliant blue skies, summer crops are harvested, all of nature has a "crisp edge."

...A TIME of busy activity — teachers organize classrooms and make plans, families prepare for a new school year, school buses run and car pools begin, classrooms and hallways are filled with excited children, playgrounds resound with laughter.

...A TIME of newness — starting a new school year, buying new shoes and new book bags, meeting new people, making new friends, learning more about the big, wonderful world.

All of this and more is the excitement of September! Watch students' smiles widen and their eyes brighten as they enter your "come alive" classroom. Your classroom will say "Welcome, I'm glad you're here!" from the ceiling to the floor, from windows and doors, from work sheets and activity projects, from stories and books, and especially from you — an enthusiastic, "project planned" teacher!

This little book of SEPTEMBER PATTERNS, PROJECTS & PLANS has been put together with tender loving care to help you be prepared to meet every one of the school days in September with special treats, learning projects and fun surprises that will make your students eager to participate in every phase of the daily schedule and look forward to the next day. Best of all, the patterns, projects and plans are ready for quick and easy use and require no elaborate materials and very little advance preparation.

For your convenience, the materials in this book have been organized around four major unit themes. Each of the patterns, projects and plans can be used independently of the unit plan, however, to be just as effective in classrooms in which teachers choose not to use a unit approach. All are planned to complement and enrich adopted curriculum schemes and to meet young children's interests and learning needs.

Major unit themes include:

- September Surprises
- Off To School We Go!
- Learning And Growing/Life Skills
- Johnny Appleseed

Each unit includes a major objective and things to do; poster/booklet cover, bulletin board or display; patterns; art and/or an assembly project; reproducible basic skills activities; and book, story and poem suggestions to make the literature connection.

Other topics, special days and events for which patterns, projects and plans have been provided include:

- Grandparents' Day (September 11)
- Citizenship Day (September 17)
- Good Neighbor Day (September 25)
- Self-Awareness
- School Safety
- Community Helpers
- First Day of Autumn

SEPTEMBER SURPRISES

Major Objective:
Children will develop awareness of the colors, sights, sounds, special days and events that characterize the month of September.

Things To Do:

- Use the patterns in this book to make decorations for doors, windows, desks, etc.

- Have the children complete the activity on page 16. Ask the children who do not have grandparents to choose special friends for this activity!

- In celebration of the first day of autumn (September 21), have the children make autumn leaf mobiles (page 32).

- Celebrate Native American Day (September 23) by letting the children make Indian bead necklaces (page 20)!

- Reproduce pages 28-30 for the class. Instruct each child to cut the pages apart, staple them together, and follow the directions to make autumn colors books.

- Send the "letter to parents" (page 10) home to announce the month's plans and to ask for donations for your materials collection. Check your supplies to be sure you are ready for the month!

- Read *A Day of Autumn* and *Fall Is Here* (see page 78).

To complete the activities in this book, you will need:

- construction paper (assorted colors)
- crayons & markers
- paste
- scissors
- tape
- paper clips
- thread
- stapler
- clothes iron

- small tree branches & leaves (for leaf mobiles, pg. 32)
- brads
- apples (see Johnny Appleseed unit)
- ingredients for apple recipes (pg. 74)
- ingredients for fake clay (pg. 20)
- toothpicks
- wax paper
- hole punch

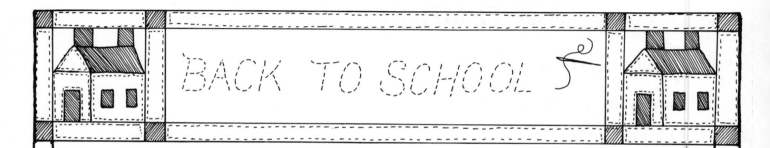
BACK TO SCHOOL

Dear Parents,

September is such an exciting month! For teachers and children, it's a month of change and new beginnings — new surroundings, new friends, new experiences, new skills and new challenges.

This month your child will explore the world of learning and will develop many new basic skills. Encourage your child to practice and develop these new skills at home. During the coming weeks, we will begin to:

- follow directions
- read and write our ABC's
- identify community helpers
- develop a broader understanding of the world around us

- work and play together
- count and compute
- practice good citizenship
- question and experiment

Please take time to discuss each school day with your child. Ask open-ended questions and offer positive feedback. Review all work brought home and set aside a special place for displaying the work. Your constant interest will play an important part in your child's learning success.

In order to help with our projects, you can donate ribbon, fabric scraps, egg cartons, gift-wrap and other "goodies" for our materials collection. Perhaps you can think of other materials that would afford us creative learning experiences. If so, please send them with instructions for their use.

I am glad to have your child in my class, and I am looking forward to a wonderful school year. I hope you will visit often to share in the growth and excitement taking place in our classroom.

Sincerely,

SEPTEMBER ALPHABET

A...A,B,C,D,E,F,G,H,I,J,K,L,M,N,O,P,Q,R,S,T,U,V,W,X,Y,Z!
B...Books to read
C...Calendars and clocks
D...Days are getting shorter
E...Exciting beginnings
F...First signs of fall
G...Grandparents' Day and Good Neighbor Day
H...Hooray for September!
I...It's time to learn!
J...Johnny Appleseed's birthday
K...Kicking piles of leaves!
L...Labor Day
M...Making friends
N...Names, numbers and numerals
O...Open windows to let breezes in
P...Pencils, paper, paint and paste
Q...Quiet time to relax and rest
R...Ready to learn
S...School days, school days
T...Telling time
U...Unexpected changes in nature
V...Vacations end, school begins
W...Warm days linger
X...X-ercise and outdoor play
Y...Yippee! Leaves are falling!
Z...Zooming into fall!

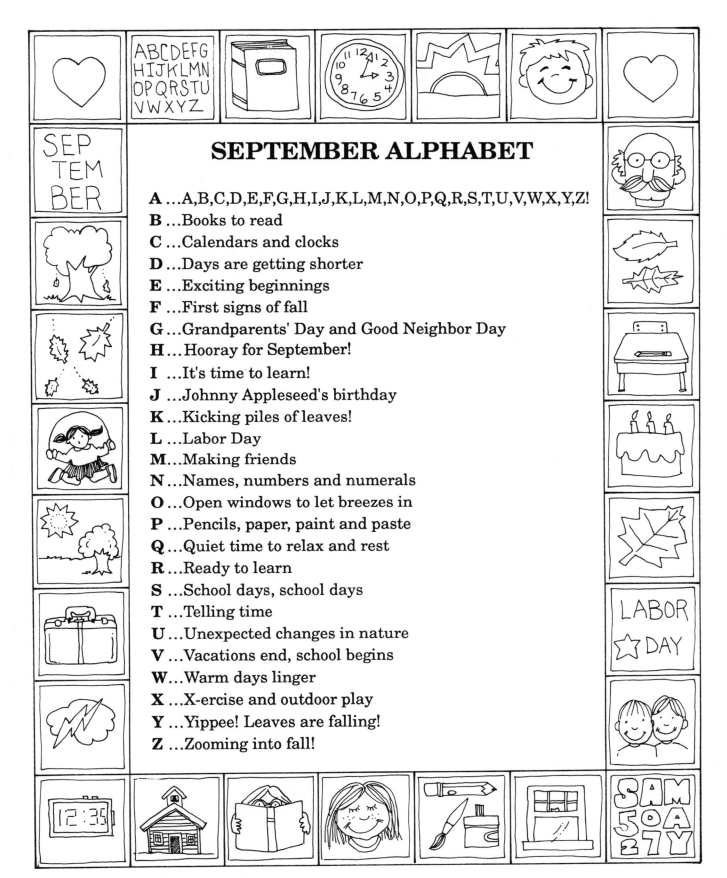

SEPTEMBER CLASSROOM
MANAGEMENT CHART

SEPTEMBER

Name _____

SEPTEMBER SURPRISES WHEEL

Color the pictures below.
Cut and paste each picture in the correct space on the *September Surprises* wheel.

Name _____

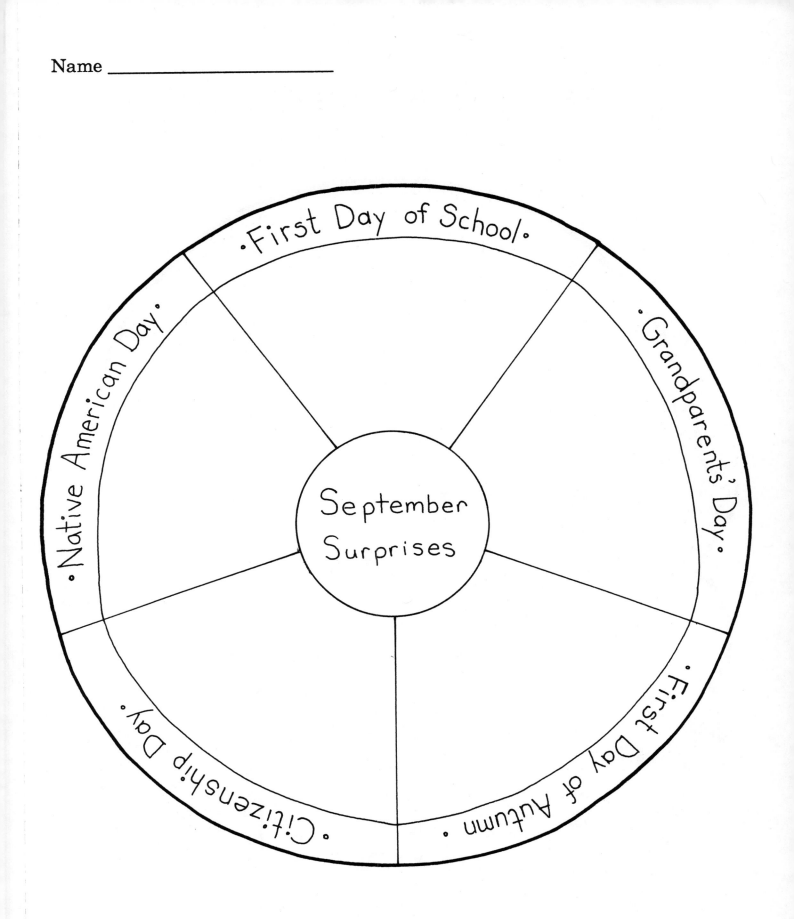

GRANDPARENTS' DAY BASKET

Draw pictures to fill the basket with things you would like to give your grandparents for Grandparents' Day.

HAPPY GRANDPARENTS' DAY!

TO:

FROM:

Creative expression
©1989 by Incentive Publications, Inc., Nashville, TN.

Name _____

PICNIC TIME

Color the pictures of three
good citizens.
Circle the pictures of three
poor citizens.

Critical thinking
©1989 by Incentive Publications, Inc., Nashville, TN.

GOOD CITIZENSHIP AWARDS

I respect the rights and property of others.

‡cut

I am a good citizen. ☆

cut

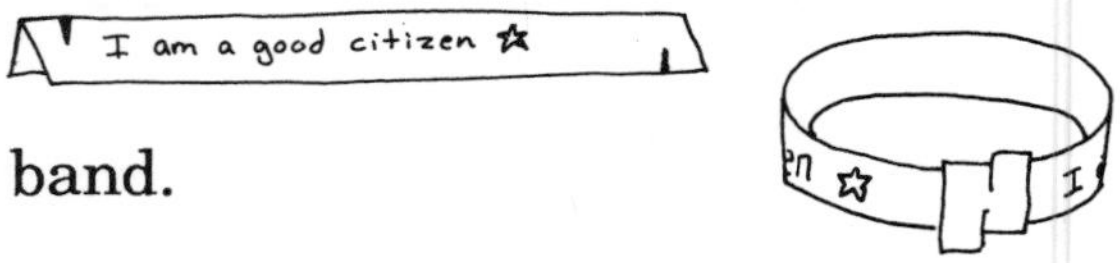

cut

I am a good citizen ☆

1. Color and cut out the good citizenship wrist band.
2. Fold along the dotted lines.
3. Cut where indicated and assemble the wrist band around the child's arm.

_____

respects the rights and property of others by:

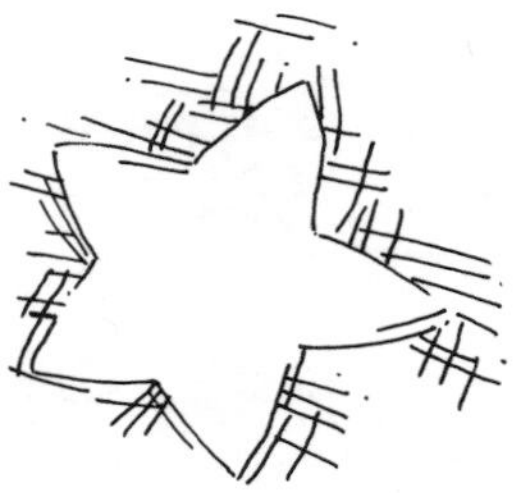

_____   taking turns

_____   being quiet at quiet time

_____   treating classmates fairly

_____   not pushing or shoving

_____   not touching the property of others without
            permission

_____   not littering

_____   sharing

_____
signed

_____
date

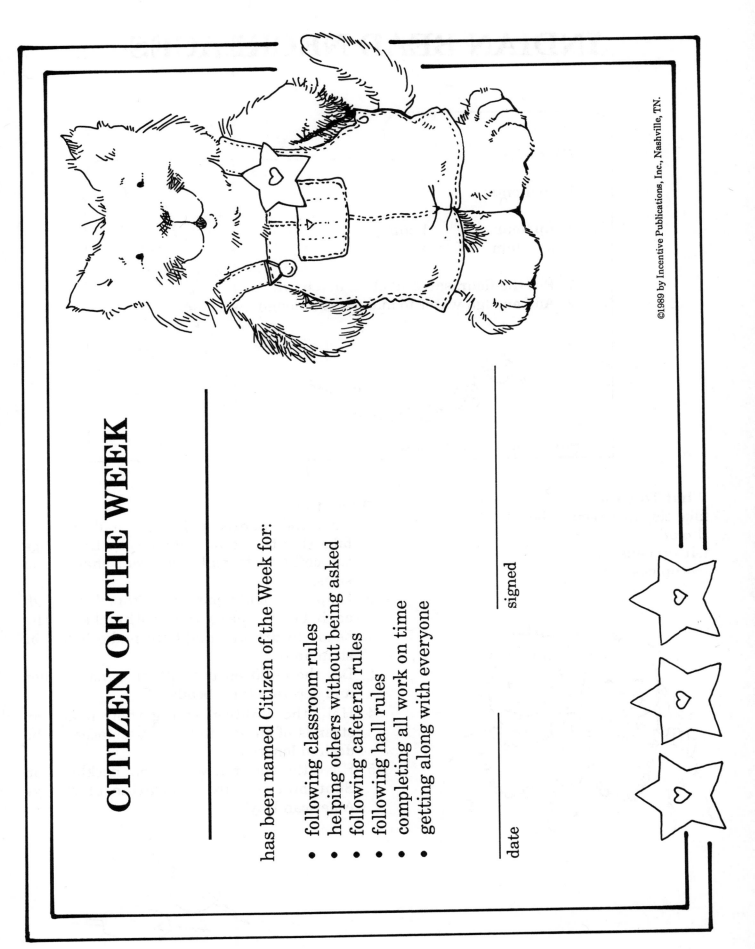

CITIZEN OF THE WEEK

_____

has been named Citizen of the Week for:

- following classroom rules
- helping others without being asked
- following cafeteria rules
- following hall rules
- completing all work on time
- getting along with everyone

_____
date

_____
signed

INDIAN BEAD NECKLACES

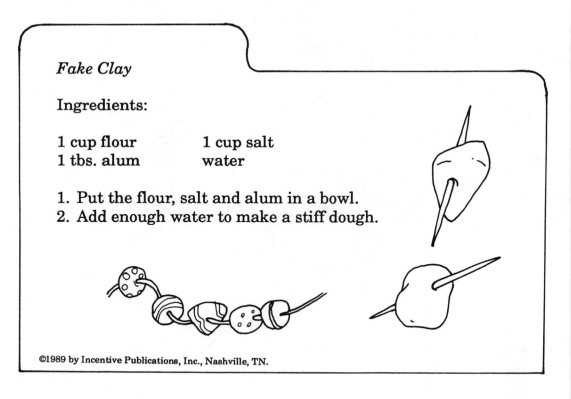

Fake Clay

Ingredients:

1 cup flour   1 cup salt
1 tbs. alum   water

1. Put the flour, salt and alum in a bowl.
2. Add enough water to make a stiff dough.

What To Use:
fake clay (see recipe above)
thread
felt-tip pens
toothpicks

What To Do:
1. Have the children pinch off small pieces of fake clay to use to make beads. Encourage the children to make different shapes and sizes.
2. Help each child push a toothpick through each bead. Leave the toothpicks in the beads to dry overnight (to make holes for stringing).
3. Let the children use felt-tip pens to color and decorate their beads.
4. Help the children string their beads on strands of thread to make necklaces of the desired lengths.
5. Have the children wear their necklaces on September 23 in celebration of Native American Day!

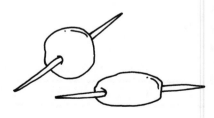

A CARD FOR A GOOD NEIGHBOR

Make a card for a good neighbor.
Address the card and mail it!

cut

fold

stamp

Construction:

1. Reproduce the patterns on pages 23 - 25 and cut them out of construction paper or color them with markers.
2. Cut the caption "On The Lookout For The First Signs Of Autumn" out of construction paper.
3. Have the children draw and cut additional symbols out of construction paper.
4. Assemble the board as shown above.

Variation:

• Omit the autumn symbols and substitute any one of these captions:

- • *On The Lookout For Good Work*
- • *On The Lookout For Good Manners*
- • *On The Lookout For Good Health Habits*

Add the appropriate symbols and projects to the board.

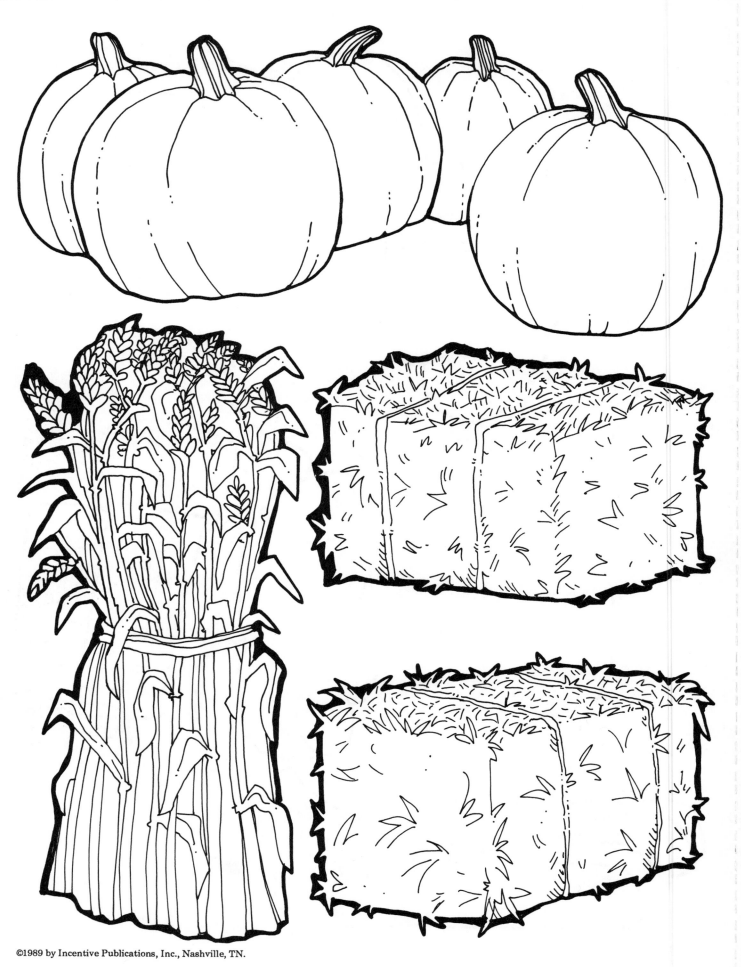

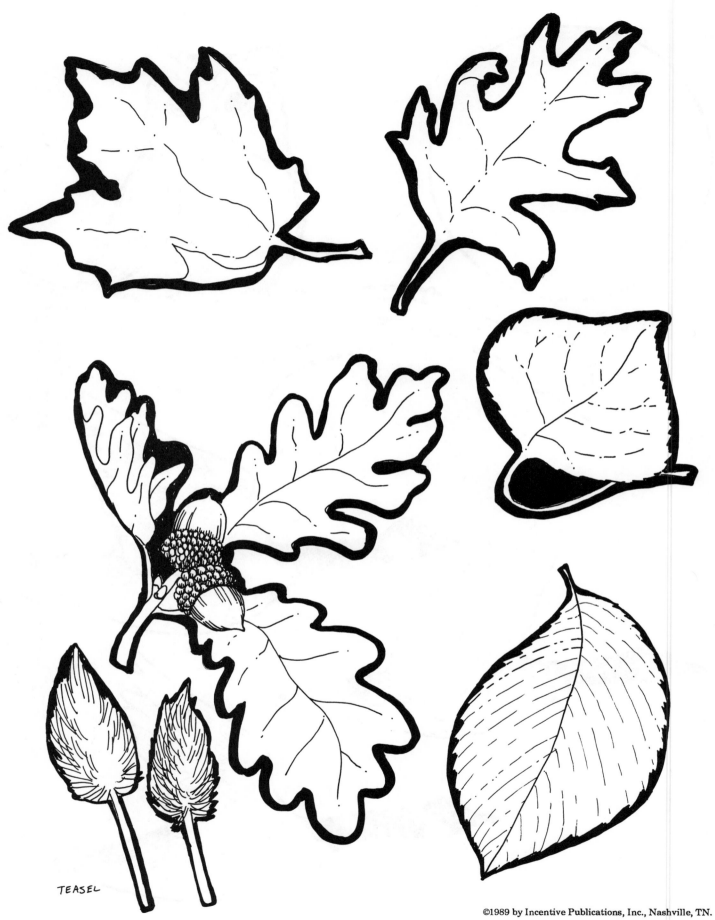

TEASEL

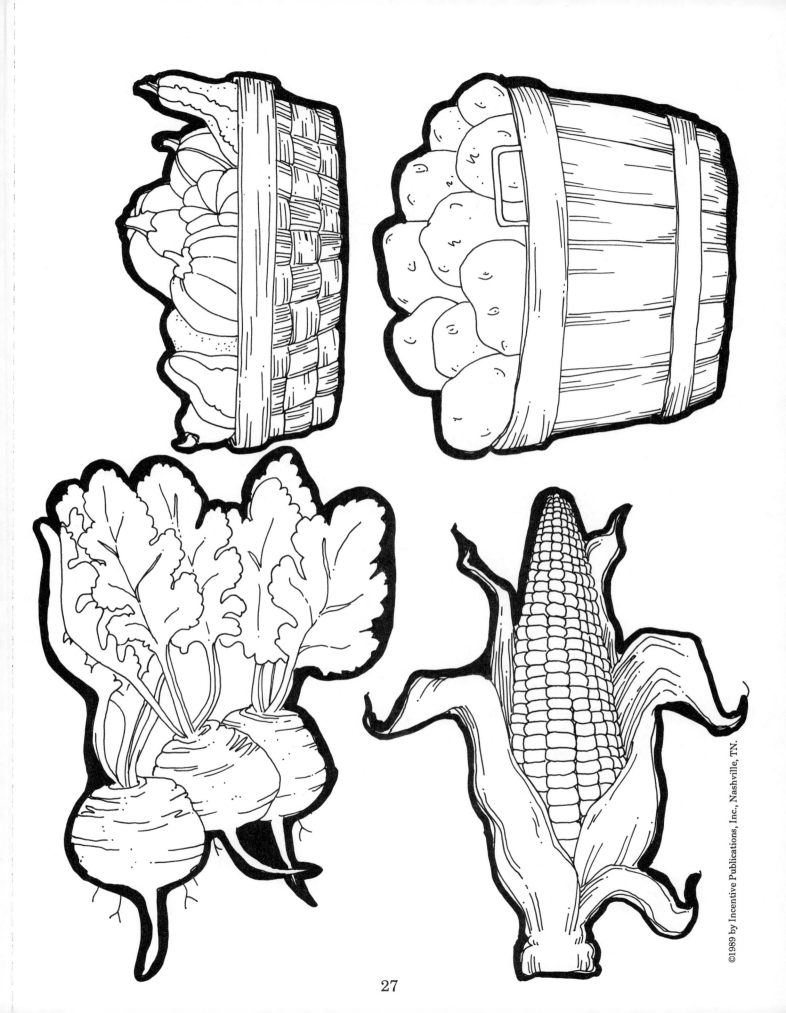

MY AUTUMN COLORS BOOK

By _____

- -

Color the picture.

Autumn colors,
Red and orange
Yellow and brown,
Autumn colors
All around.

Find something yellow.
Color every 5 yellow.
Color every 6 black.

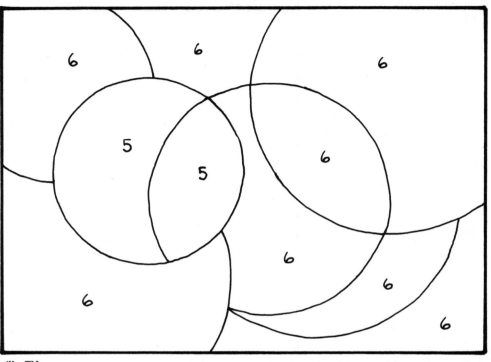

Find something brown.
Color every 7 brown.
Color every 8 green.

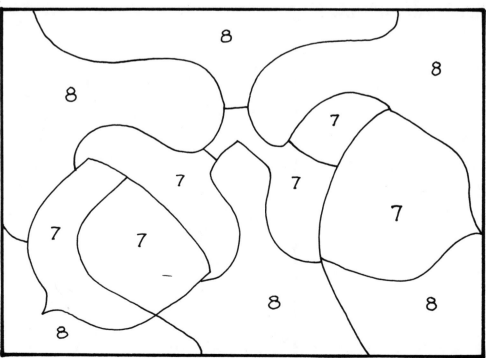

Find something red.
Color every 1 red.
Color every 2 brown.

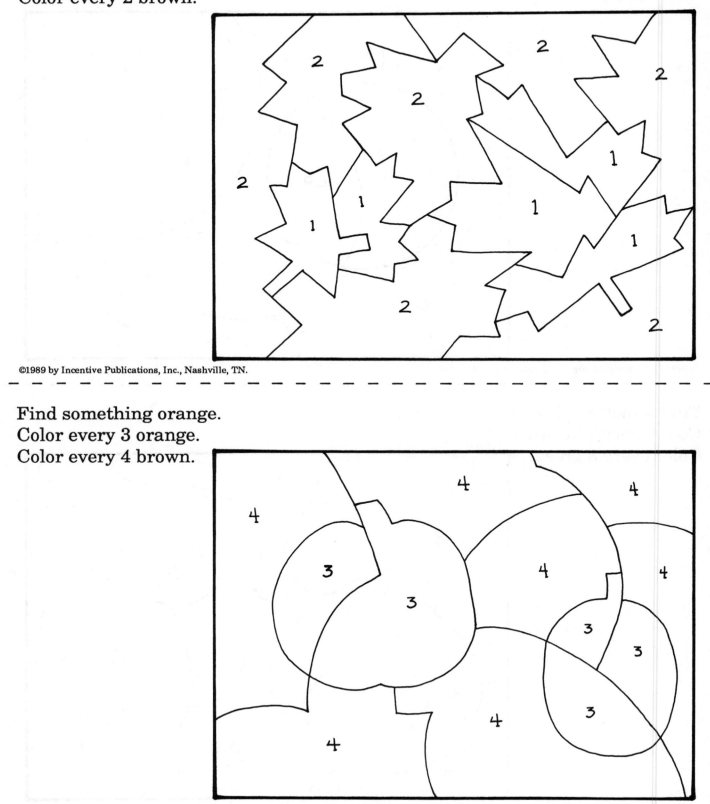

Find something orange.
Color every 3 orange.
Color every 4 brown.

AUTUMN COLORS

Color each crayon the correct color.

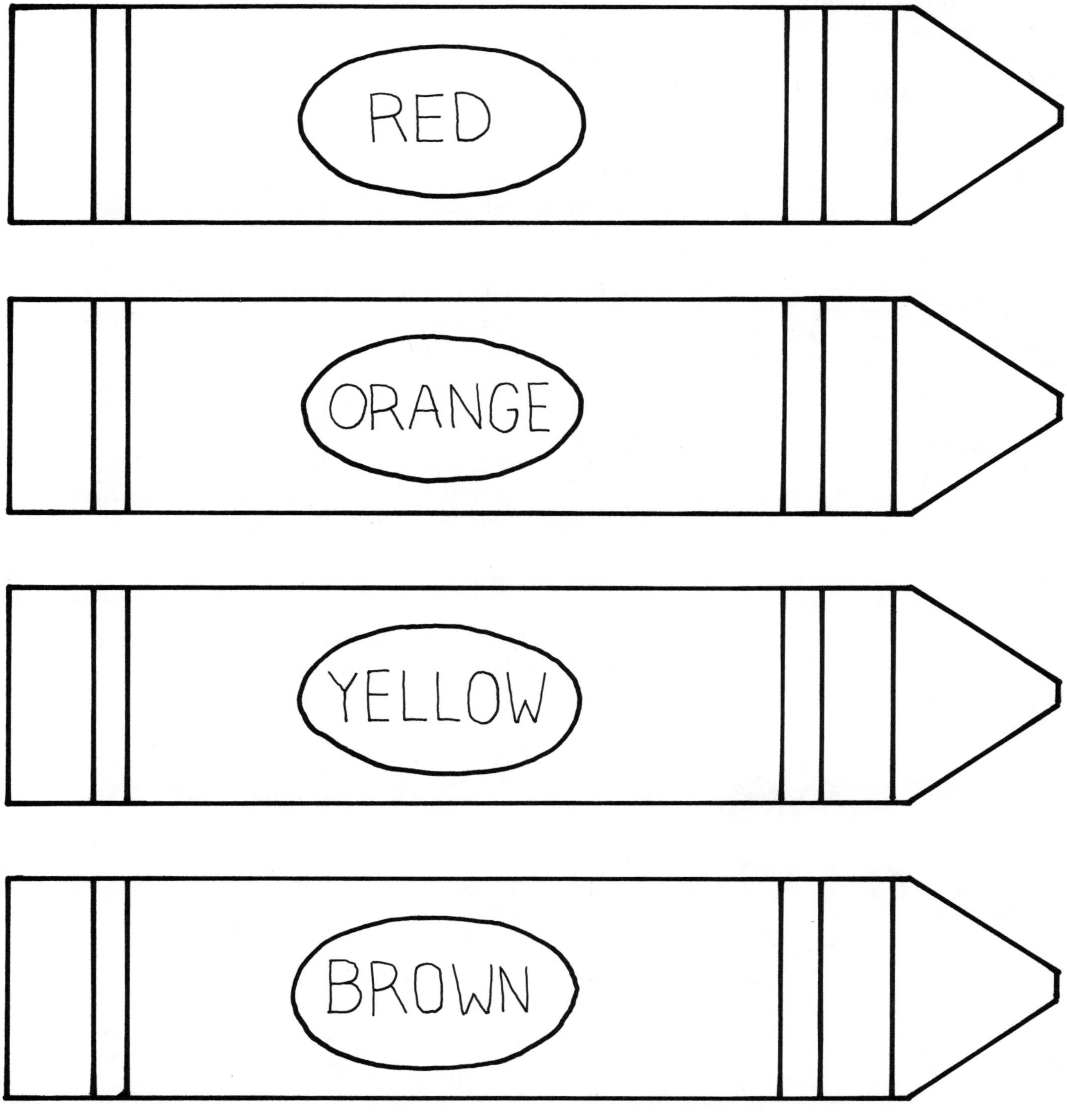

RED

ORANGE

YELLOW

BROWN

AUTUMN LEAF MOBILES

Children will enjoy using autumn leaves to make colorful mobiles for the classroom! After completing the activity, read *A Tree Is Nice* (see page 78) to make the literature connection.

What To Use:

leaves
wax paper
warm iron
scissors

hole punch
thread
small tree branches

What To Do:

1. Let the children collect leaves outside for this activity.
2. Instruct each child to place one leaf at a time between two sheets of wax paper. Help each child press a warm iron over the leaf (obviously, adult help is needed for this step).
3. Help the children cut around their leaves, making sure that a paper border remains for hanging the leaf.
4. Have the children punch a hole in the border of each leaf and push thread through the hole to make a loop for hanging.
5. Help the children hang their leaves from small tree branches.

Note: If leaves are not available, cut leaves out of autumn colors of construction paper!

OFF TO SCHOOL WE GO!

Major Objective:
Children will develop awareness of and appreciation for the privileges and responsibilities inherent to the school community.

Things To Do:
- Construct the bulletin board on page 34. When it's time to take down the pictures, put each child's picture and samples of the child's work in a folder (date the work sheets). At the end of the school year, ask the children to draw pictures of themselves again. Add the new pictures and samples of the children's most recent work to the folders. Staple each child's material together to make a booklet.

- Invite community helpers to visit the class. Let each child draw a picture of the hat that the community helper he or she would most like to be might wear (see page 47). Display the hats on a bulletin board with the caption "Many Hats To Wear."

- Have the children make designs by cutting various shapes out of construction paper, wallpaper, fabric, etc. to paste on tagboard squares. Ask each child to tell what his or her favorite shape is.

- Take the class on a shape scavenger hunt. Name a shape and ask the children to point out as many objects of that shape as they can.

- Let one week be "safety" week. Each day discuss important safety rules for the classroom, school grounds, playground, neighborhood and home. After discussing traffic signs and their meanings, have the children color and cut out the patterns on page 45 and use them in "talks" about traffic safety. At the end of the week, present each child with a safety specialist certificate (page 44).

- Send a copy of the alphabet practice sheet (page 49) home with each child. Instruct parents to use the practice sheet as they help their children at home.

- String a clothesline along a wall or under the chalkboard. Provide clothespins and allow the children to hang their work on the line.

- Read *Leo The Late Bloomer* and *Rosa-Too-Little* (see page 78) to make the literature connection.

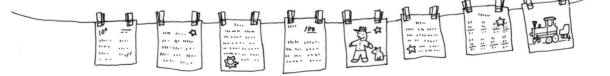

Construction:

1. Reproduce the picture frame pattern on page 35 in quantities to meet the needs of the class.
2. Have the children draw pictures of themselves in the picture frames. (You draw one of yourself, too!)
3. Cut the caption "Here We Are!" out of construction paper.
4. Assemble the board as shown.

Variation:

- Ask the children to bring baby pictures of themselves from home to tape in the picture frames (do not have the children write their names). Give the children one week to guess whose picture is whose. (This is a great ice breaker for a "first" parent meeting or conference!) Later, let the children draw their own "self-portraits" to add to the board. Substitute the caption "Look How We Have Grown!"

Here is _

CLASSROOM HELPERS

TEACHER'S HELPER

Dear _____,
Welcome to school!
I'm glad you are
in my class!

_____   _____
Teacher   Date

My teacher
is proud of
me because

_____

NAME TAG

sits here.

OFF TO SCHOOL

Cut out the pictures below and paste them in the correct boxes to tell a story.

Name _____

FACES SHOW FEELINGS

Draw faces on the children to show how they feel. Andy forgot his book. Today is Sally's birthday. Susan has a stomachache.

SCHOOL BUS

Expressing emotions
©1989 by Incentive Publications, Inc., Nashville, TN.

SCHOOL BUS

SCHOOL BUS

GOOD
STUFF

· GOOD QUALITY WRITING ·
PAPER

LUNCH TIME!

MY BAG!

PINK PEARL
ERASER

BEST BUNNY TALES

WRITTEN & ILLUSTRATED BY
MEGAN MARIE

Name _____

GETTING ORGANIZED

Cut and paste the pictures in the correct containers.

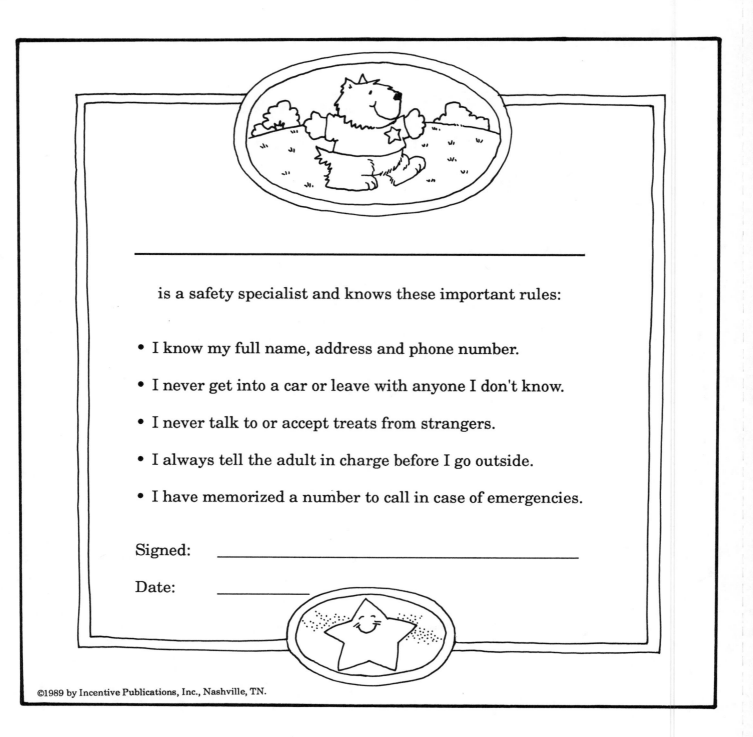

_____

    is a safety specialist and knows these important rules:

- I know my full name, address and phone number.

- I never get into a car or leave with anyone I don't know.

- I never talk to or accept treats from strangers.

- I always tell the adult in charge before I go outside.

- I have memorized a number to call in case of emergencies.

Signed: _____

Date: _____

IS ^

SAFETY SPECIALIST

HELPERS AND THEIR TOOLS

Draw a line to connect each community helper with the correct tool.
Can you describe each person's job?

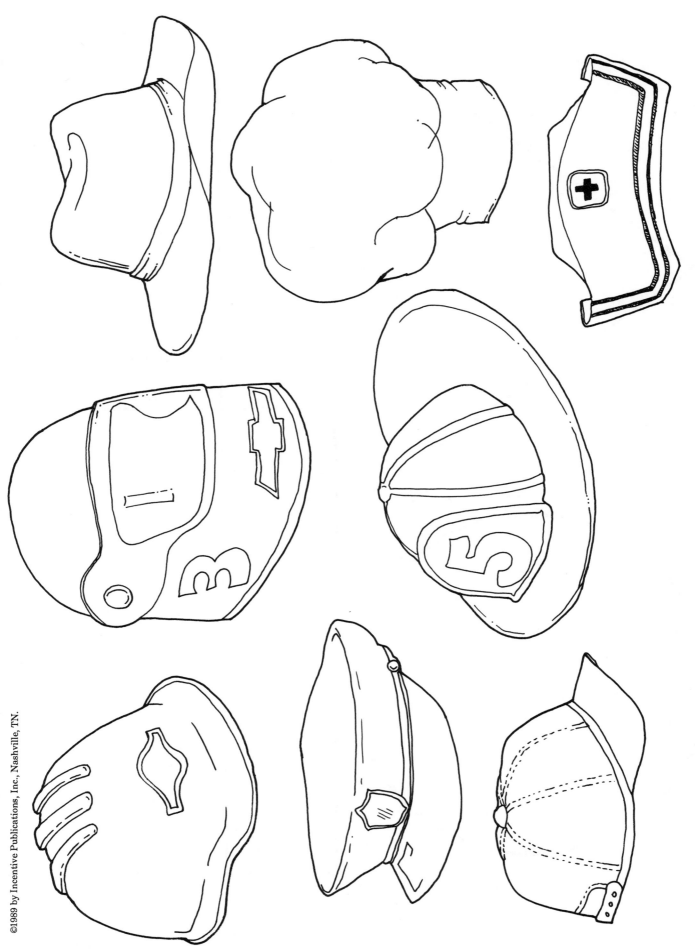

Name _____

ALPHABET PRACTICE CHART

Trace the letters.

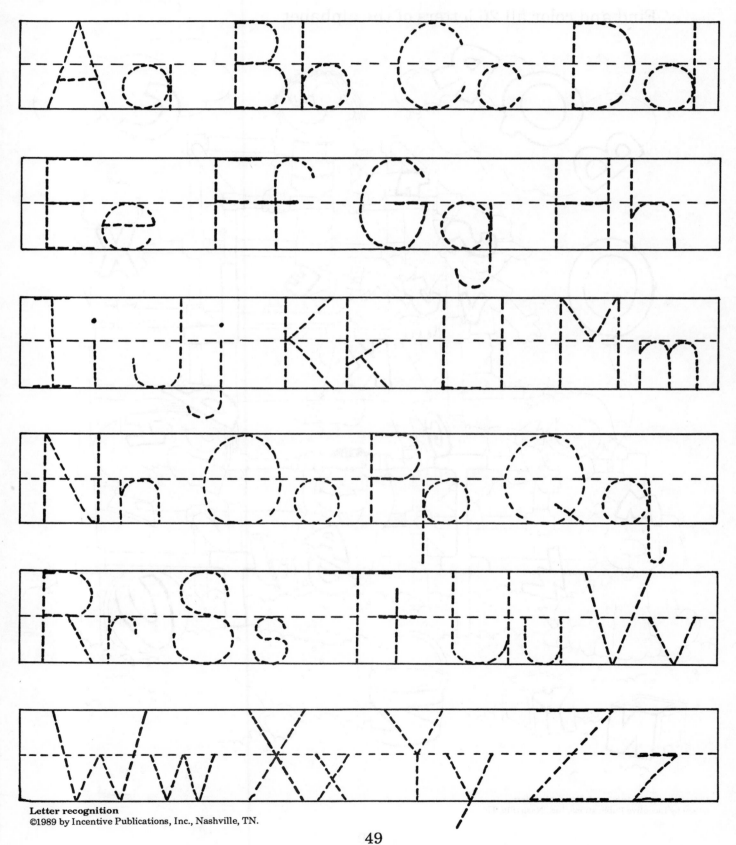

Name _____

ALPHABET SEARCH

Find and color all 26 letters of the alphabet.

Letter recognition/visual discrimination
©1989 by Incentive Publications, Inc., Nashville, TN.

BIRTHDAY TIME

Cut and paste the correct number of candles on the cake to show
how old you will be on your next birthday.

Construction:
1. Reproduce the patterns on pages 53 and 54 (you will need a boxcar for each child), and cut them out of construction paper or color them with markers.
2. Write "Birthday Express" on the engine.
3. Write each child's name, birthday and the age that the child will be on his or her next birthday on a boxcar as shown.
4. Cut the caption "Our Birthday Express" out of construction paper.
5. Assemble the board as shown above.

Variations:
- Use the patterns to make an "Alphabet Express" to display above a chalkboard or on a wall. Print a letter of the alphabet on each boxcar.
- Substitute the caption "All Aboard The Citizenship Express." Have each child write his or her name on a boxcar. Write "good citizenship" rules on a chart and display it on the board (see the "Citizen of the Week" award on page 19).

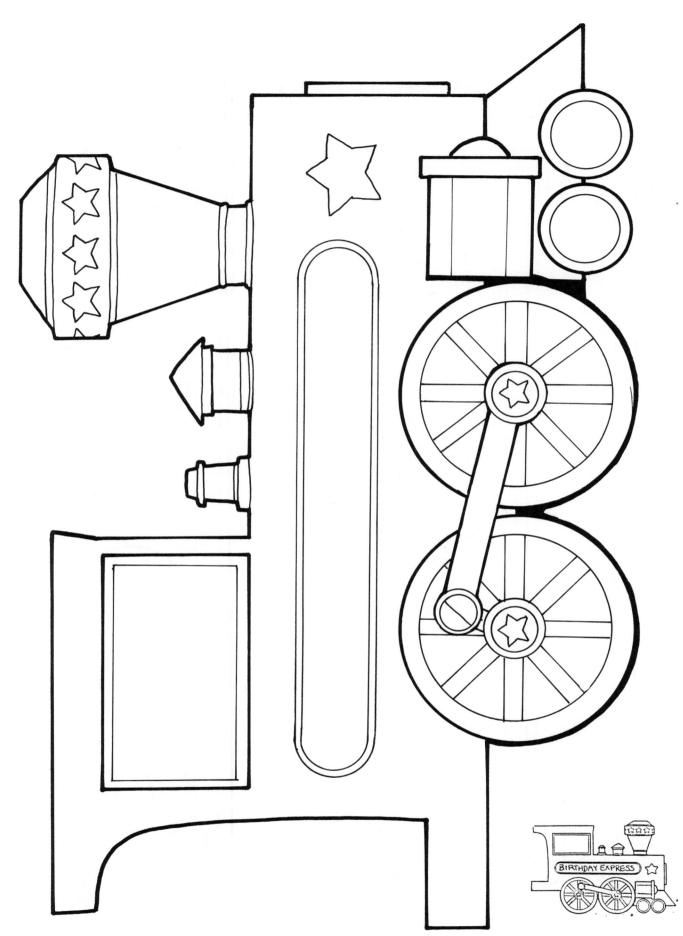

BIRTHDAY EXPRESS

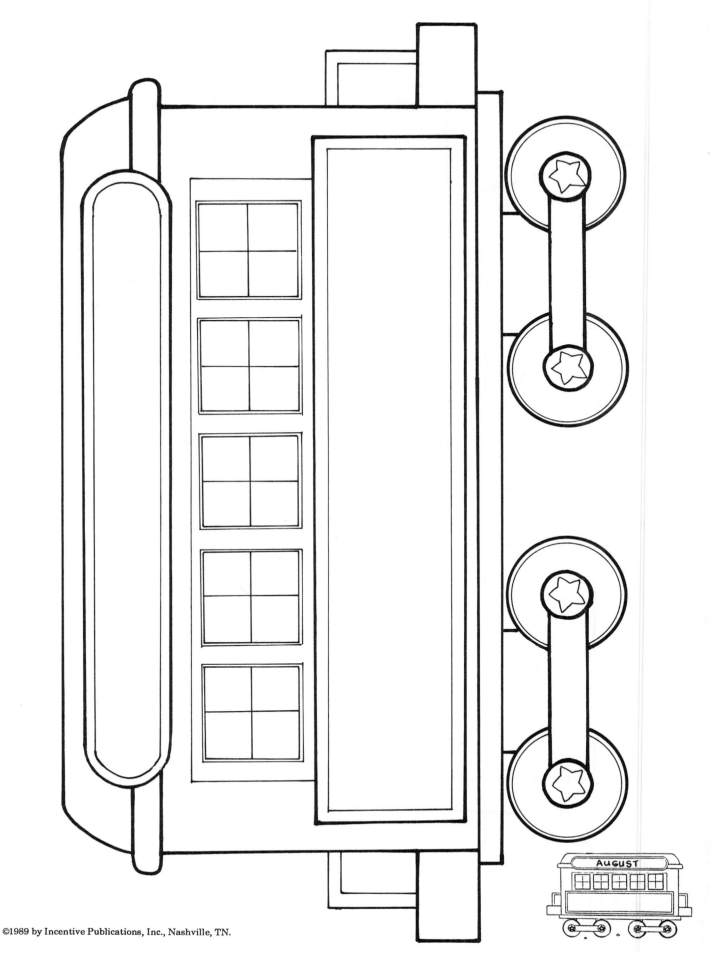

LEARNING AND GROWING/LIFE SKILLS

Major Objective:
Children will become familiar with various kinds of clocks and watches, will gain an understanding of different times of day and daily schedules, and will learn to use the calendar, telephone and money.

Things To Do:

The Calendar
- Choose a special place to put the monthly calendar. Let the children mark each day by writing the date in the correct square. You may choose to write the date on a calendar symbol as well as use calendar symbols to mark special days (see page 58).

Telling Time
- Use the patterns on pages 60 and 61 to construct a large clock (attach hands with a brad). Before each study time or scheduled activity, help a child move the hands to show the correct time. Have the children say the time aloud.

- Reproduce the pattern on page 60 in quantities to meet the needs of the class. Have the children trace the numerals and say each one aloud. Assign each child a time of the school day to "show" on the clock and to illustrate in some way on a sheet of paper. Display the clocks and drawings on a bulletin board with the caption "A Day At School."

- Let the children examine both a digital and standard clock. Talk about the differences. Set the clocks for the same time and have the children read the time shown on each. Change the time and repeat the activity.

- Draw several clocks on the chalkboard, each showing a different time (all with big hands pointing to 12). Ask a child to circle the numeral that each little hand is pointing to and to say the time shown on each clock. Change the times and repeat the activity with another child.

- Show the children how to set an alarm clock and allow them to take turns setting the clock. Set the alarm to ring before lunch, recess and dismissal time.

The Telephone

- Make a list of the children's names and telephone numbers on the chalkboard (have the children supply their numbers verbally). Then make a list for each child. Help the children staple their directories together and add construction paper covers. Send the directories home with the children for year-long use!

- Reproduce the telephone pattern (page 63) in quantities to meet the needs of the class. Help each child write his or her telephone number on a phone. Repeat this activity periodically until the children can write their numbers independently.

- Have the children memorize their parents' work numbers, the number of someone to call if their parents cannot be reached, and important emergency numbers.

Money

- Set up a play store in a corner of the room. Put price tags on the items. Provide the children with play money to use in make-believe shopping experiences.

- Give each child a container to decorate and use as a bank (coffee can, plastic box, jar, etc.). Let the children take their banks home and begin filling them with coins!

- Play the missing coin game. Line up several coins and ask the children to hide their eyes. Take away one of the coins and have the children tell which coin is missing.

- Share *Anno's Counting Book* and *Over In The Meadow* (see page 78).

SEPTEMBER

Sunday	Monday	Tuesday	Wednesday	Thursday	Friday	Saturday

HOW TO USE THE SEPTEMBER CALENDAR

Use the calendar to:

...find on what day of the week the first day of September falls
...count the number of days in September
...find the number on the calendar which represents September
...mark the birthdays of "September babies" in your room
...mark special days

- Labor Day (first Monday in September)
- Grandparents' Day (September 11)
- Rosh Hashanah (Jewish New Year - September 12)
- Citizenship Day (September 17)
- Native American Day (September 23)
- Good Neighbor Day (September 25)
- Johnny Appleseed's Birthday (September 26)

Teach the children this rhyme!

Thirty days hath September   *Excepting February alone,*
April, June and November;   *And that has twenty-eight days clear*
All the rest have thirty-one,   *And twenty-nine in each leap year.*

CALENDAR ART

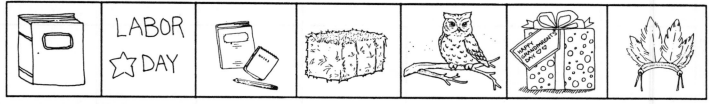

THE CLOCK

There's a neat little clock,
    In the schoolroom it stands,
And it points to the time
    With its two little hands.

And may we, like the clock,
    Keep a face clean and bright,
With hands ever ready
    To do what is right.

WRIST WATCHES TO WEAR

What To Use:
construction paper
crayons and markers
scissors
tape or paper clips

What To Do:
1. Reproduce the wrist watch pattern below in quantities to meet the needs of the class.
2. Have each child cut a wrist watch out of construction paper and/or color it with crayons and markers.
3. Help the children write the numerals on their watch faces and draw hands pointing to their favorite times of day.
4. Tape or paper clip the watches around the children's wrists and have each child tell why the time shown on his or her watch is a favorite time of day.

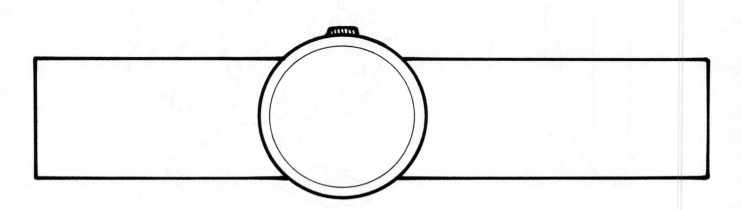

PLAY AND LEARN MONEY

JOHNNY APPLESEED

Major Objective:
Children will become aware of the folklore associated with Johnny Appleseed and will develop appreciation for the contributions that seeds, fruits and trees make to daily life.

Things To Do:

- Give each child an apple. Ask the children to examine the apples and to supply words or phrases that describe how the apples look, feel, smell and taste (have the children bite their apples!). List the words on the chalkboard. This is a good motivator for the bulletin board on page 66.

- Construct the bulletin board on page 66 and use the caption "On The Lookout For Seeds." Have each child decorate a small paper bag with pictures of seeds and trees. Send a note home with each child asking parents to help the child collect seeds in the bag. Add some of the seeds to the board; plant the other seeds and watch them grow!

- Cut an apple in half and show the children the "star" in the center. Give each child an apple half (remove the seeds). Mix a thin red tempera wash. Let the children dip their apple halves in the paint and make "star" prints on white paper. After the paint dries, fold the papers in half to make cards, or display the prints on a bulletin board.

- Discuss ways that seeds are spread. Bring a milkweed seedpod to class and demonstrate how the seed's "parachute" causes it to blow in the wind.

- Paste the leaf and seed patterns (page 75) on index cards and have the children match the leaves and seeds.

- Grow your own salad! "Plant" parsley on a sponge soaked in water and place the sponge on a flat dish. The parsley grows quickly and is fun to watch!

- Place the following on a science table: apple pie, sliced apple, applesauce, apple juice, and apple jelly. Have the children observe the items daily to watch as mold develops.

Construction:

1. Reproduce the patterns on pages 67 - 69 and cut them out of construction paper or color them with markers.
2. Cut the caption "Johnny Appleseed Planted Seeds Everywhere He Went!" out of construction paper.
3. Assemble the board as shown above.

Variations:

- Tell the story of Johnny Appleseed. Provide story starters and ask the children to make up stories about adventures that Johnny Appleseed might have had.

  Examples: The day Johnny Appleseed met the grizzly bear...
  Johnny Appleseed curled up inside the dark cave to wait for the storm to pass and...

- Give each child a quarter of an apple to eat. Ask the children to save the apple seeds. Paste the apple seeds on the path behind Johnny Appleseed!

Johnny Appleseed

APPLE SEEDS

BULLETIN BOARD BORDER

1. FOLD PAPER ACCORDION STYLE.

2. CUT OUT APPLE ON SOLID LINES. (DO NOT CUT ON DOTTED LINES.)

3. OPEN.

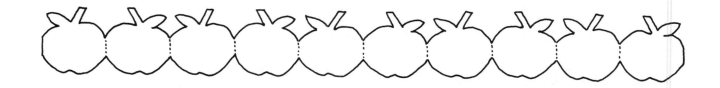

Name _____

JOHNNY APPLESEED

Color the pictures and tell the story.

A seed is planted.

A tree sprouts and grows.

The tree sprouts leaves and then blossoms.

The tree bears apples to eat!

ALIKE OR DIFFERENT?

Color the two apples that are alike.

Color the two apple pies that are alike.

Color the candied apple that is different.

Recognizing similarities & differences
©1989 by Incentive Publications, Inc., Nashville, TN.

APPLE PUZZLERS

1. Reproduce the puzzles below in quantities to meet the needs of the class.
2. Cut the puzzles apart and put a set of puzzles in an envelope for each child.
3. Have the children match each picture with the correct word(s).

Note: The apple puzzles also can be used as an independent activity.

APPLE RECIPES WITH A SCIENCE BONUS

Apple Juice

2 cups apples, seeded and cut into small pieces
4 cups water
1/4 cup sugar

Mix all ingredients. Put 1/2 of mixture in blender and blend well. Add the rest of mixture and blend.
©1989 by Incentive Publications, Inc., Nashville, TN.

- This is a good activity to demonstrate how a solid is turned into a liquid.

Dried Apples

apples   salt   water

Peel and core apples. Cut apples into thin rings and soak rings in salty water for 30 minutes. Spread apple rings on a cookie sheet and cover with a thin sheet of gauze (to protect the apples from bugs). Place apple rings in a sunny spot and let dry for two weeks.
©1989 by Incentive Publications, Inc., Nashville, TN.

- Check on the apple rings every few days and disucss the changes taking place. This activity allows the children to observe the changes in appearance, texture and taste.

Applesauce

apples   water   cinnamon
sugar   lemon juice

Cut apples into small pieces (leave peelings on) and put them in an electric frying pan. Add a little sugar and lemon juice to taste. Cover apples with water. Simmer until completely disintegrated. Mash mixture with wooden spoon. Add dash of cinnamon.
©1989 by Incentive Publications, Inc., Nashville, TN.

- Let the children taste the applesauce and discuss the experience. Ask questions such as: "Did we add enough sugar?" "What did the lemon juice do to the mixture?" "Why did the apples become mushy?" "Is our applesauce as good as the canned applesauce sold in grocery stores?"

74

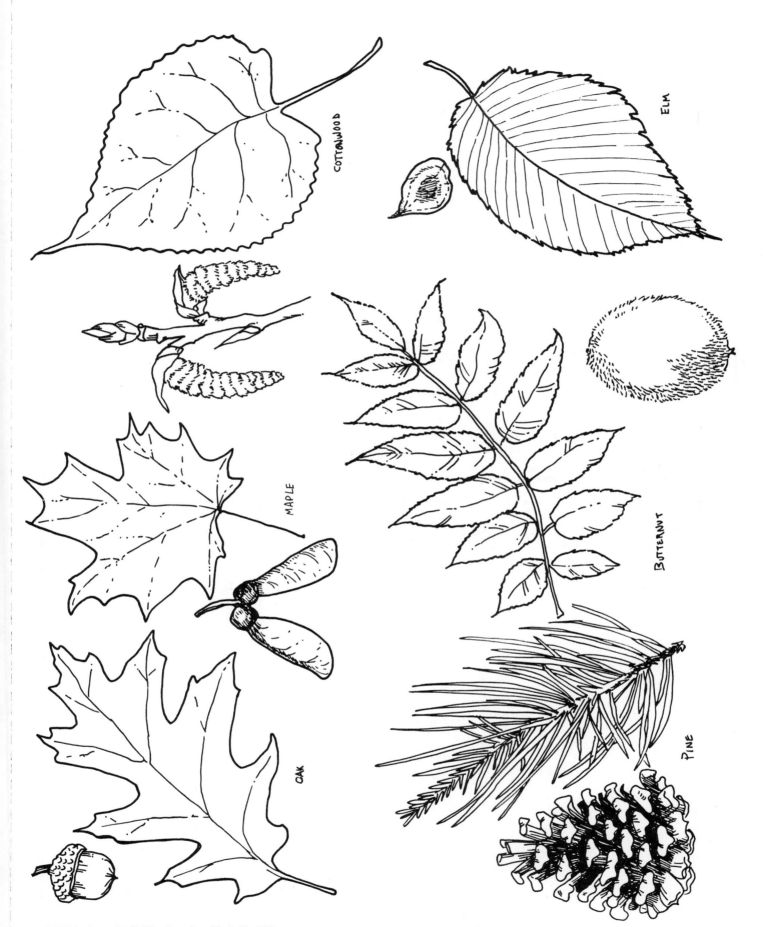

COTTONWOOD

ELM

MAPLE

BUTTERNUT

OAK

PINE

Apple of the Day Award

To : _____

For: _____

Teacher: _____

Date : _____

A note from the teacher's desk...

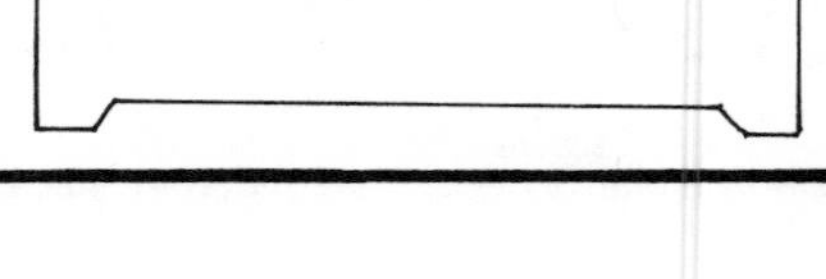

apple muffin

applesauce

apple pie

candied apple

basket of apples

apple juice

BIBLIOGRAPHY

Anno's Counting Book. Mitsumasa Anno. Thomas Y. Crowell, Co.
This book teaches the concept of zero, the numerals 1-12, and the concepts of groups and sets using illustrations of a growing village through the 12 months.

A Book of Seasons. Alice and Martin Provensen. Random House.
A simple text and beautiful illustrations portray seasonal changes in a manner sure to capture and hold children's attention.

A Day of Autumn. Betty Miles and Marjorie Auerbach. Alfred A. Knopf.
This poetic description of the sights, sounds, smells and feelings of an autumn day is perfect for September reading.

Fall Is Here! Jane Belk Moncure. The Child's World, Inc.
This book describes in verse the various activities and changes associated with the fall. The simple text and full-page illustrations make it perfect for young children.

Grandfather Twilight. Barbara Berger. Putnam.
Soft, glowing illustrations accompany this simple story of twilight personified as a gentle grandfather.

Leo The Late Bloomer. Robert Kraus. Windmill Books.
A small tiger reassures young learners that it is all right to learn to read, write and do other things at your own rate.

Let's Be Enemies. Janice May Udry. Harper & Row.
This story about the ups and downs of friendship helps children develop an understanding of themselves and others.

Over In The Meadow. Olive A. Wadsworth. Scholastic.
This is a delightful counting book to sing!

Rosa-Too-Little. Sue Felt. Doubleday.
A little girl named Rosa experiences joy and pride after she finally learns to write her name and thus receive a library card of her very own.

A Tree Is Nice. Janice May Udry. Harper & Row.
Bold and colorful illustrations are predominant in this book which focuses on trees and their uses.

What I Did Last Summer. Jack Prelutsky. Greenwillow Books.
This collection of humorous poems about summer activities will make children laugh with delight.

INDEX